ABDO Publishing Company

FISH & GAME

WALLEYED PIKE

Sheila Griffin Llanas

visit us at
www.abdopublishing.com

Published by ABDO Publishing Company, PO Box 398166, Minneapolis, MN 55439.
Copyright © 2014 by Abdo Consulting Group, Inc. International copyrights reserved in all
countries. No part of this book may be reproduced in any form without written permission from the
publisher. The Checkerboard Library™ is a trademark and logo of ABDO Publishing Company.

Printed in the United States of America, North Mankato, Minnesota.
112013
012014

 PRINTED ON RECYCLED PAPER

Cover Photo: Engbretson Underwater Photography
Interior Photos: Alamy pp. 9, 21, 26, 29; AP Images pp. 7, 22, 23;
    Engbretson Underwater Photography pp. 1, 5, 11, 13, 14, 17, 19; iStockphoto p. 25

Editors: Rochelle Baltzer, Megan M. Gunderson, Bridget O'Brien
Art Direction: Neil Klinepier

Library of Congress Cataloging-in-Publication Data

Llanas, Sheila Griffin, 1958- author.
  Walleyed pike / Sheila Griffin Llanas.
       pages cm. -- (Fish & game)
  Includes index.
  ISBN 978-1-62403-109-0
1. Walleye (Fish)--Juvenile literature. 2. Pike fishing--Juvenile literature. I. Title.
  QL638.P4L59 2014
  597'.758--dc23
                         2013028915

Contents

Walleye! 4

History 6

In Balance. 8

Teeth to Tail 10

Senses 12

Habitat 14

Diet. 16

Life Cycle 18

Walleye Season 20

Got One! 24

Day's End 28

Glossary 30

Web Sites 31

Index. 32

Walleye!

Walleyed pike avoid the sun. They seek out dark, deep waters. They hide near rocks, weeds, and sunken trees. And, they take advantage of cloudy days.

Anglers know cloudy days and clear nights make good walleyed pike fishing times. Walleyed pike, or walleye, are strong swimmers. Caught on a hook, they shake their heads hard! They give anglers an exciting adventure.

Walleye come with another reward, too. They are one of the best-tasting freshwater fish. The fish are easy to fillet and cook. And, walleye meat is white and flaky.

A prize walleye can weigh more than 20 pounds (9 kg). The world record stands at 25 pounds (11 kg). Caught in Tennessee in 1960, that lunker measured 41 inches (104 cm) long!

The walleye is the official state fish of Minnesota, Vermont, and South Dakota. Many states celebrate walleye with giant statues and billboards! Good sport and good eating make walleye a favorite of anglers all over the United States and Canada.

Walleyed pike are also known as pike, pickerel, pike perch, and jack salmon.

History

Walleye are native to the middle United States. Originally, they were found between the Rocky and Appalachian Mountains. They swam in great numbers in the Great Lakes.

For some native Great Lakes peoples, fish meant survival. Setting out in canoes, they lit torches for light. Then they speared the fish or caught them in nets.

When Europeans arrived, they fished for profit and sport. Many species were overfished, and populations began to shrink.

To preserve this valuable resource, fish **hatcheries** opened in the 1800s. After walleye **fry** hatched, they were placed in rivers and lakes. The young walleye restored populations in native waters.

WILD FACTS!

Blue pike, a walleye subspecies, once thrived in Lakes Erie and Ontario. Today, they are believed to be extinct due to pollution and overfishing.

Walleye were placed in nonnative waters, too. They showed up in Arizona in 1957 and Washington in 1962. Montana's first known walleye was netted in 1989. These walleye offered exciting new fishing opportunities. Yet they also changed nonnative **habitats**.

Walleye fry are so small more than 1 million of them can fit in a single bag!

In Balance

In nonnative waters, walleye altered the existing balance. In Canyon Ferry Reservoir in Montana, walleye fed heavily on perch and trout. Those native species grew scarce. For a few years, trout fishing was grim.

Montana wanted to keep walleye. Yet the state also valued its trout and perch. Fish managers had to restore balance. They stocked full-grown trout, which were too large for walleye to eat. And, they raised the walleye daily catch limit.

Today, walleye stocking is a common practice. Walleye are grown in **hatcheries**. **Fry** are placed into waters as needed.

It can take a lot of fry to stock one lake. In Indiana, almost 540,000 baby walleye are slipped into Lake Monroe every year. Minnesota hatcheries grow up to 5

When walleye fry are ready, they are transported to their release site.

million walleye **fingerlings** each year. In turn, Minnesota anglers catch up to 3.5 million walleye every year!

Walleye fishing is big business for good reason. It is fun! To keep it fun for everyone, be a responsible angler.

Every state has different guidelines. Rules vary for boats, bait, and **bag limits**. Before heading out to fish, study state fishing rules. Apply for a fishing license. Get good maps. And most of all, learn to think like a walleye.

WALLEYED PIKE TAXONOMY:

Kingdom: Animalia
Phylum: Chordata
Class: Actinopterygii
Order: Perciformes
Family: Percidae
Genus: *Sander*
Species: *S. vitreus*

Teeth to Tail

More than 6,000 species of fish belong to the order Perciformes. About 165 of those species belong to the perch family. Walleye are the largest members of this family.

Walleye usually weigh 4 to 22 pounds (2 to 10 kg). They reach lengths of 12 to 36 inches (30 to 90 cm). For many anglers, a walleye measuring more than 14 inches (36 cm) long is a keeper.

The walleye's scale-covered body is long and thin. Its mouth is filled with many teeth! This freshwater fish is brownish-green or silver on top with a creamy white belly. Walleye also have seven to nine dark stripes, or saddles.

Walleye use their fins for swimming. They flap their fins to move and balance. The front dorsal fin has 12 to 16 sharp spines. The back dorsal has soft rays. The caudal fin has a **unique** white spot on the bottom tip.

The Walleyed Pike

SPINY DORSAL FIN

SOFT DORSAL FIN

CAUDAL FIN

EYE

MOUTH

PELVIC FINS

PECTORAL FIN

ANAL FIN

Senses

Walleye behavior is all about light. Their shiny, marble-shaped eyes are their best-known feature! They give walleye keen vision in dark waters.

There is a reason walleye eyes are so sensitive to light. Each eye has a tapetum lucidum. This reflective layer of pigment makes everything brighter.

The tapetum lucidum gives walleye a kind of night vision. In dark waters, other fish can't see as well. This gives walleye the advantage as predators. Seeing clearly in the dark, they swoop in to catch their prey.

Walleye also see colors. Researchers believe that orange, yellow, and yellow-green stand out for these fish. That is useful information for anglers when choosing lures.

WILD FACTS!

The tapetum lucidum is what makes cats' eyes glow in the dark.

The walleye's species name refers to its eyes. Vitreus means "glassy."

Habitat

Walleye huddle against sunken trees, boulders, and weed beds.

Today, walleye thrive in lakes, ponds, rivers, and streams. They are found from northern Canada to the southern United States. Walleye prefer cool freshwater at temperatures below 77 degrees Fahrenheit (25°C).

To escape the sun, walleye swim as deep as 60 feet (18 m) below the surface. They seek dark

North America

Europe

Asia

Africa

South America

Australia

■ Where walleyed pike live

habitats where they can hide from the light. In winter, thick ice and layers of snow shield them from the sun.

In murky waters, walleye stay more active in the daytime. They like to feed in choppy water. In clear waters, they wait until night to feed in shallow areas. Anglers keep these habits in mind when fishing for walleye.

Diet

Adult walleye are mainly piscivores, or fish-eaters. Their diet consists of minnows, freshwater drum, and rainbow smelt. Walleye in Arizona feast on threadfin shad. In Montana, they eat yellow perch, suckers, and trout. Walleye also prey on crayfish, snails, and insects. They suck in prey and grip it in their fanglike teeth.

Walleye are top predators. They hunt prey in low light, especially at dawn and dusk. Since walleye can see in almost total darkness, they continue to feed into the night. Walleye rely on being able to see better than their prey.

Walleye never stop growing. They must eat year-round, even in winter. Ice slows them down, but it does not stop them from feeding. Anglers attract them with live bait or lively artificial lures.

WILD FACTS!

Walleye often hang out in loose schools.

Sometimes in summer, walleye have more than enough food available to eat. They swim right past anglers' bait!

Life Cycle

When winter ice breaks up, walleye prepare to **spawn**. Spring weather warms the water. Spawning reaches its peak in waters of 42 to 50 degrees Fahrenheit (6 to 10°C). Walleye are not nesting fish. Many seek rocky areas near falls or dams for spawning.

The female can release more than 400,000 eggs. She does this at night. Then, two males **fertilize** the area. Walleye do not care for their eggs or young.

The eggs are sticky. Clinging to rocks, gravel, or weeds helps shelter them. Each egg measures just one-sixteenth of an inch (0.2 cm) across.

After about two weeks, the eggs hatch. The tiny fish are one-fourth of an inch (0.6 cm) long. They float around, nibbling on **zooplankton**. After another two

WILD FACTS!

Many walleye return to their birthplace to spawn.

weeks, the young walleye spread out into open water. Here, many become food for other fish.

Those that survive grow fast. By fall, young walleye measure a healthy 6 inches (15 cm). By their second summer, males reach 12 inches (30 cm) long. By the third summer, females are 13 to 14 inches (33 to 36 cm) long. At four years old, this rapid growth rate slows.

Male walleye are mature at age two to four. Female walleye are mature between ages three and six.

Walleye Season

Anglers have their favorite times of year to fish. But states make the laws. Responsible sportsmen check all the rules before casting a line.

Walleye are valued for summer and winter fishing. In states such as Nebraska and Ohio, walleye fishing is open year-round. Some anglers prefer to fish just before or during the walleye **spawn**.

Other anglers think the post-spawn is the best time to hook a trophy. In Minnesota, walleye season starts in mid-May, after walleye spawn. At this time, adult females are very hungry! On the prowl for food, they strike at the bait anglers offer them.

Lake walleye reach keeper size, about one pound (0.5 kg), in three years.

night crawlers

No matter what the season, some of the best walleye fishing happens in low light. Sudden loss of light triggers walleye to bite! When the sun goes down or dark clouds roll in, walleye start feeding.

Anglers choose bait based on experience and recommendations. Some swear by squiggly night crawlers. Others choose leeches. Ribbon leeches, with firm bodies, are excellent walleye bait.

Minnows are a favorite baitfish. Some people think female minnows work better than male minnows. This may be due to color. Male minnows have black heads. Females have more silver, which may attract walleye.

Anglers must put safety first. They always wear life preservers. They have basic first-aid kits and wear sunscreen and bug spray for protection.

When using artificial lures, anglers consider the walleye's favorite colors. They fill their tackle boxes with bright green and orange.

Walleye anglers can fish from a boat, a dock, or the shore. From any location, there are two tricks for catching walleye. One is to get the lure or bait presentation to hit the water's rocky bottom. The other is to fish slowly and patiently.

Got One!

Anglers rely on other equipment besides live bait. Some use slip bobbers, which float on the water's surface. They stop the line at a certain length. This lets anglers keep the bait just at the bottom's surface. That bait will look alive, dangling in front of a hungry fish!

A jig is made up of a hook and plastic or live bait. These come in colors and shapes walleye are likely to notice. Some plastic baits also contain scents. This helps mask the angler's scent and put out attractive scents for the walleye. Crankbaits are another option. They look and act like the fish walleye like to eat.

A spinning rod and reel are must-haves for walleye seekers. The upper part of the rod should be very sensitive to movement. That way, the angler knows if a walleye is nibbling.

WILD FACTS!

The sauger is a close relative of the walleye. The two fish look very similar, but only the walleye has a white spot on the caudal fin.

If the line tugs, the angler waits. A cautious walleye might only be testing the bait. When it takes the bait into its mouth completely, the line pulls harder. When the fish is hooked, the angler reels it in and scoops it from the water with a net.

Sometimes, fishing requires teamwork!

Holding a fish takes practice. Stay away from the walleye's teeth and strong jaws. Instead, grip the walleye behind the head, with a finger and thumb on either side.

Anglers are careful not to touch the walleye's gills or eyes. This would harm the fish.

Next, decide whether to keep the fish or put it back. Know the state's limits. For example, the daily catch limit in Missouri is four. Any walleye under 15 inches (38 cm) must be released. In Ohio, the same length is required, but the daily limit may vary throughout the year.

Some walleye anglers carry a weight chart in the boat. Without one, they can still estimate a walleye's weight. They use a tape measure and do a little math.

Anglers measure the length of the fish. Then they use the equation length times length times length divided by 2,700. For example, a 15-inch walleye weighs approximately $15 \times 15 \times 15 / 2700$, or 1.25 pounds (0.6 kg).

When catch-and-release fishing, keep the fish in good health. Keep the walleye wet as much as possible. If the fish is not moving, hold it underwater. Gently wave it back and forth. This moves water through the gills to help it breathe. When the fish revives, let it swim away.

Day's End

At the end of the day, clean up! It shows respect for nature and for fellow anglers. Take everything you brought. Leave everything that was already at the location.

This includes water. Carrying water to another lake risks infecting the new lake with an **invasive** species. Before leaving a water access, clean and drain water from the boat.

The same rules apply to live bait. Never dump unused leeches, worms, or minnows in the water. Nonnative bait species can invade and harm the local **environment**. Dispose of unused live bait properly according to local rules.

Loss of **habitat**, pollution, and overfishing have caused problems for walleye and other fish. Fish managers and anglers share a common goal to keep walleye safe and healthy. Protecting a fish that is fun to catch and tasty to eat is good for the **environment**. And, it keeps fishing fun!

Anglers find walleye fishing both exciting and relaxing! This activity provides healthy time outdoors with friends and family.

Glossary

bag limit - a usually daily limit on the number of fish an angler may keep.

environment - all the surroundings that affect the growth and well-being of a living thing.

fertilize - to make fertile. Something that is fertile is capable of growing or developing.

fingerling - a young fish usually about two inches (5 cm) long, or about the length of a finger.

fry - young fish that are not yet big enough to be fingerlings.

habitat - a place where a living thing is naturally found.

hatchery - a place for hatching eggs.

invasive - tending to spread.

spawn - to produce or deposit eggs.

unique (yoo-NEEK) - being the only one of its kind.

zooplankton - small animals that float in a body of water.

Web Sites

To learn more about walleyed pike, visit ABDO Publishing Company online. Web sites about walleyed pike are listed on our Book Links page. These links are routinely monitored and updated to provide the most current information available.

www.abdopublishing.com

Index

A
Arizona 7, 16

B
bait 9, 16, 20, 22, 23, 24, 25, 28
bobber 24

C
Canada 5, 14
catch and release 27
color 10, 11

D
diet 8, 15, 16, 18, 20, 22, 24

E
eggs 18
eyes 12

F
fingerlings 9
fins 10, 11
fishing 4, 5, 6, 7, 8, 9, 10, 12,
    15, 16, 20, 22, 23, 24,
    25, 27, 28
fishing line 20, 24, 25
fry 6, 8

G
gills 27

H
habitat 4, 7, 14, 15, 18, 23, 28
hatchery 6, 8, 9
history 4, 6, 7, 8
hook 4, 24

I
Indiana 8
invasive species 28

J
jig 24

L
license 9
limits 8, 9, 27
lure 12, 16, 23

M
Minnesota 5, 8, 9, 20
Missouri 27
Montana 7, 8, 16
mouth 10, 25

N
Nebraska 20
net 6, 25

O
Ohio 20, 27

P
Perciformes (order) 10
predators 19
prey 12, 16

R
reel 24
reproduction 18, 20
rod 24

S
scales 10
senses 12, 16, 22, 23, 24
size 4, 10, 16, 18, 19, 27
South Dakota 5
spines 11
stocking 6, 7, 8

T
tapetum lucidum 12
teeth 10, 16, 26
Tennessee 4
threats 6, 28

V
Vermont 5

W
Washington 7
weight 4, 10, 27